Restoration in The Valley

Rediscovering Your Truth

"Finding Purpose in the Valley: Navigating Life's Depths to Discover Your True Calling"

Moya Martin

Copyright © 2024

All Rights Reserved

Dedication

This book was written directly for individuals who are somehow stuck on their journey towards fulfillment or simply looking for a path of redirection and soul reflection. The chapters in this book are not written to enforce or mislead the masses into believing there is such a thing as rapid transformation but rather to portray guiding tools and directions for you to create an individualized and adjustable plan for your healing journey.

Acknowledgement

This endeavor could not have been possible without the vision and grace of God. I am undoubtedly grateful for my life's journey and the experiences that forged the path to share valuable lessons and inspirations from overcoming them.

Special thanks to my family, relatives, and friends who stood firm with me on my path of transformation, accepted my unique attributes, and allowed me the space and time I needed to shift and redirect my focus toward my soul's fulfilling purpose.

I am grateful for the leaders and life coaches I had the opportunity to learn from, whether through direct interaction or observation from afar, whose words inspired me to push through some of my hardest days. Their guidance has been a driving force and a constant mental replay, reminding me never to give up. Those words taught me that hope and faith transition into eventually realizing your purpose. Thanks to those who shared the words, "There's greatness in you," even before I could see it within myself.

Special thanks to Alpha Book Writers, Jenna West & April Woods, my dedicated project manager, my editorial team, and Matthew Garvy Sr., publishing and marketing consultant. And to all the other staff members who contributed to making this book a success, thank you.

I also want to give special thanks in advance to everyone who picks up this book and takes the time to read through its pages. To those who engage with the suggested activities, know that we share a common path toward enlightenment and fulfillment. It is with great pleasure that I remind you that you are uniquely made, valued, and respected in the Creator's eyes. May you design your personalized plan to match your unique life path.

Cheers to your illuminated and successful transition!

Contents

Dedication iii

Acknowledgment iv

Introduction vii

Chapter 1 Fear and Success 1

Chapter 2 Self-Awareness 5

Chapter 3 Purpose 10

Chapter 4 Goals 12

Chapter 5 Growth 14

Chapter 6 Relationships 16

Chapter 7 Health and Well-being 18

Chapter 8 Resilience 22

Chapter 9 Living Authentically 25

Chapter 10 Making a Positive Impact 28

About The Author 30

Introduction

This book explores the concept of restoration amidst life's challenges and setbacks, linking difficult times to a valley where transformation and renewal can occur. Despite facing adversaries, I draw strength from my experiences and stage a path for personal evolution and healing.

Through insights and profound reflections, readers are encouraged to embrace introspection, self-awareness, and resilience as they navigate their own valleys. This book offers strategies for finding hope, rediscovering purpose, and sharing valuable insights with you. The valley is not a place of punishment but rather a necessity, ultimately experiencing restoration amidst adversity.

"Finding Purpose in the Valley" is not just about weathering the storms of life; it's about harnessing the power of adversity to uncover the deeper meaning behind our experiences. It's about recognizing that the valley is not a place of despair but a fertile ground for growth and renewal.

So, if you find yourself amidst the shadows of a valley, uncertain of the path ahead, know that you are not alone. Within these pages, you will find guidance, inspiration, and the reassurance that even in the darkest of times, purpose and meaning await your discovery.

Chapter 1
Fear and Success

Fear is a powerful emotion that can affect us in various ways. It can arise from perceived threats, uncertainty, or situations outside our comfort zones. While fear can sometimes serve as a protective mechanism, helping us avoid danger, it can also hold us back from reaching our full potential and experiencing the fullest of life. Fear can lead to division, prejudice, and conflict, hindering progress and understanding among people.

Acknowledging and understanding our fears is the first step in overcoming them. By shining a light on our fears, you can begin to examine their root causes and evaluate whether they are rational or irrational. This self-awareness allows you to develop strategies for managing fears and moving forward despite them.

Facing our fears often requires courage and resilience. It involves stepping out of our comfort zones, taking risks, and embracing uncertainty. However, it's important to remember that growth and personal development often occur outside our comfort zones.

By sharing our truths with others, we can gain perspective, encouragement, and guidance, which can empower us to confront our fears and take positive steps toward overcoming them.

Ultimately, while fear may be a natural part of the human experience, it doesn't have to control us. By acknowledging our fears, seeking support when needed, and taking proactive steps toward facing them, we can learn to live more courageously and authentically.

Success can be defined as reaching one's truest potential. Activating a balance between your physical, spiritual, and mental lifestyle thus leads to a level of peace obtained through freedom. True success begins when you fully emerge into one's truest nature, and you begin to walk in alignment with your calling, surrendering and stepping out in faith to serve others. Putting the time and effort into mastering your skills, each step leads you closer to a more fulfilling lifestyle. You must do away with the fiction of success and its attachments to money and the material world. The truth is once you are in alignment and balance, you naturally attract all the resources that you'll need to fulfill your purpose.

Life is a journey, and as the seasons unfold throughout

the years, so do we as humans. Our journey mirrors the changing seasons, with each phase bringing its own lessons and growth opportunities. Just as flowers bloom in spring, we, too, have the potential for growth and renewal. Taking responsibility for our choices and the direction of our lives is crucial, for our beliefs shape our reality. Being mindful of what you feed your mind and heart is essential, as it determines what blossoms within us.

Our minds are complex landscapes that run on unconscious patterns where personal thoughts mingle with societal norms, familial dynamics, and cultural influences. These factors can create deep-seated beliefs that may hinder our sense of worthiness and abundance.

Recognizing these influences and becoming aware of how they shape our beliefs is vital to personal growth and empowerment. By examining our thought patterns and the roots of our beliefs, we gain the opportunity to challenge and redefine them, paving the way to fulfillment.

Cultivating strong faith, taking intentional actions, and embodying our dreams are essential components of manifesting our desired outcomes. It's a journey of self-discovery, healing, and transformation where we align our thoughts, beliefs, and actions with our true desires and aspirations. Through this alignment, we can transcend limiting beliefs and unlock our full potential for abundance and fulfillment.

The factors that mold our beliefs ultimately influence our sense of worthiness and ability to achieve abundance. Our internal thought processes and external influences both hold considerable sway in shaping how we view ourselves and our surroundings.

These internal thoughts, such as self-doubt and feelings of inadequacy, hinder our ability to recognize and pursue abundance in our lives. Negative thought patterns can act as barriers, preventing us from fully realizing our potential and achieving our goals.

On the other hand, external influences, such as societal norms, cultural expectations, and family dynamics, also exert a powerful influence on your beliefs and behaviors. The values and traditions often shape us passed down through generations, as well as the messages we receive from the media, peers, and authority figures.

Becoming aware of these influences and examining

whether they align with your true desires and values is crucial for personal growth and fulfillment. It requires a willingness to challenge ingrained beliefs and question the status quo, which can be both liberating and transformative.

Chapter 2
Self-Awareness

By cultivating self-awareness, fostering a sense of empowerment, and taking intentional action toward your goals, you can begin to rewrite your internal narratives and create a reality aligned with your desired outcomes. This process may involve letting go of limiting beliefs, embracing new perspectives, and forging a new path forward.

By aligning beliefs with our aspirations and combining faith with deliberate action, we can manifest abundance and create the life we truly desire.

Activity:
Take the time to reflect and LIST some beliefs that you have in question.

    1. Are these beliefs aligned with me now?

_____
_____
_____
_____
_____
_____
_____

2. If not, how do they affect my highest self?

_____
_____
_____
_____
_____
_____
_____

3. List some new actions/routines to replace the old ones.

_____
_____
_____
_____
_____
_____
_____

When everything around you seems chaotic and overwhelming, it's our faith, prayers, and inner resolve that guide us through. After coasting through life on autopilot, guided by unconscious beliefs, you reach a point – e.g., the midlife crisis - where you suddenly realize you're not living a fulfilling existence. Reflecting on past decisions can quickly lead to a downward spiral of regret and a desperate desire for change. It feels overwhelming, like a dense cloud hovering overhead, and every obstacle seems unreachable, surrounded by lingering deceptive memories. Life in this valley exposes unsettling and unfamiliar truths about yourself and those around you. You come face to face with your ego and the various false personas you played in the lives of others.

It dawns on you that fear has dominated your life entirely. Fear of embracing your true self. Fear of falling short of others' expectations. Fear of not belonging to your family, peers, or friends. Operating from this fear-based mentality blinds your judgment, and every decision that goes against your true desires further weighs on your soul. This deep self-reflection enables you to identify unconscious patterns, understand their origins, and choose to heal and progress, creating new cycles.

The valley isn't a punishment; it's a period of preparation. As you confront the false narrative of yourself, it also illuminates the incredible gifts and talents within you. It's a time to rediscover who you are and who you aspire to become. Isolation throughout this process catalyzes positive transformation and personal development when approached with introspection, self-awareness, and a willingness to explore new avenues in life. You've been given the chance to redirect your path and truly start living with purpose. With each action, progress, and consistent effort toward your new ideals, you gain a clearer understanding of your purpose and vision of your freedom lifestyle.

A successful life is not just about external achievements or material wealth but about finding joy, fulfillment, and meaning in every moment and aspect of your existence. Relinquishing control over factors beyond your influence, taking responsibility for your actions, remaining adaptable regardless of life's options, releasing hold of the things you can't control, taking accountability for your own actions, and physically doing the work that will get you the results. Developing a balance between releasing old patterns and cultivating new ones.

This process is not an overnight journey; you must allow yourself grace, patience and time between transitions. It's important to understand that though we live in a 3D physical plain, we are first spiritual beings. We must master the full understanding of self, our emotions, and our life paths and develop the gifts we need to harness our endurance abilities.

Self-awareness allows you to acknowledge and accept your emotions and reactions to challenges without judgment. Understanding that, it's natural to feel frustrated, disappointed, or stressed when things don't go as planned. Awareness brings about self-control. The ability to recognize and understand your own thoughts, feelings, beliefs, strengths, weaknesses, motivations, and actions. It involves being conscious of your own emotions and how they influence your behavior, as well as having insight into your values, goals, and overall identity. Self-awareness also involves recognizing how you are perceived by others and understanding how your actions impact those around you. It is a fundamental aspect of emotional intelligence and personal growth, as it allows individuals to make more informed decisions, develop healthier relationships, and navigate life's challenges more effectively. Acceptance of your feelings allows you to move forward with clarity and focus.

It's important to understand that as you become more aware of people's feelings and opinions, you don't allow your sympathetic side to differ from your own emotions. It's very easy to revert to the older patterns of people-pleasing rather than standing firm to your own survival. A good way to perceive life when you're tempted is to remember that if I'm not true and whole within myself, I'll be no good at helping others, regardless of how this new you may look and feel to the other party. Self-preservation is vital, and you must maintain focus; it may take some time, but they will eventually understand as they, too, will have to walk the path one day.

Chapter 3

Purpose

To have set objectives, we must understand "Clarity of Purpose" by understanding what we want to achieve in life and what truly matters to us. It's identifying what you want to accomplish, whether it's in your career, relationships, personal growth, or other areas. Clarity of purpose acts as a guiding light, illuminating the path ahead and providing a sense of direction. It allows you to make decisions with conviction, knowing they align with your goals and aspirations. With this clarity, you become less prone to fear and doubt, as you now have a solid foundation on which to base your choices.

From your list of introspections, you should now have a clear idea and understanding of what truly matters to you. Things beyond superficial goals, like what brings you fulfillment, meaning, and satisfaction. It may be a combination of family, creativity, making a positive impact on others, or personal growth.

Gaining Clarity of purpose enhances your confidence as your decisions now stem from a genuine knowledge of self – your strengths, weaknesses, passions, and values. When you have a deep understanding of who you are, you can approach challenges with a sense of self-assurance. Your Confidence is boosted by a profound self-awareness and a firm belief in your capacity to pursue and achieve your purpose. Knowing that you possess the skills and resources to overcome obstacles.

Understanding your purpose can also help you discover your identity. It's about recognizing your strengths, weaknesses, passions, and unique qualities that make you who you are. This self-awareness is essential for living authentically and aligning your actions with your true self.

Achieving clarity of purpose is an ongoing process that requires you to continuously ask yourself deep questions, reflect on your experiences, and be open to change and growth as you gain new insights into yourself and your goals.

- Repeat the questions and answer theory as many times as you need to uproot negative beliefs to plant and reinforce new ones.

Chapter 4
Goals

It's important to set goals but meaningful goals. You need to set goals that hold significance and value to you personally. They must be aligned with your core values, passions, and long-term vision for your life. When setting goals, it's important to consider how aligned you are with your purpose. What truly matters to you, and what will bring fulfillment and satisfaction once accomplished? It sometimes requires you to walk away from partnerships, careers, and businesses that no longer align with you.

To formulate a formula for your transformation process, your goals should be aligned and reflect who you are and where you want to go in life. To attain real solutions, you must be brutally honest with yourself. Where you are now and where you want to be. Remember, you are not your past or current situation but rather an accumulated product of the actions and decisions you take now and moving forward. When your goals are in harmony with your values and vision, you're more likely to feel motivated, inspired, and fulfilled as you work towards achieving them.

Once your fears are illuminated, you'll be able to

identify the pattern of self-doubt/ insecurity and anxiety around evolving. You'll recognize that fear is often based on perception rather than reality. From this place of knowledge and confidence, you are to acknowledge that fear is present and make the decision to confront it. You will begin to break barriers that stand in your way.

As you embark on your journey, you'll gradually witness the illusion of fear dissipate. Strength and creativity heighten, gaining momentum to follow through. Action is what brings your goals to life. By breaking them down into manageable, actionable steps and creative plans, you set the stage for progress. Taking consistent and focused action, even in the face of fear or uncertainty, is key to making progress toward your goals. Don't fall into the illusion of not having money to begin. It's best to start with the resources you have at hand, and in time, you will witness growth. It's always good to seek professional help where necessary.

Remain adaptable and flexible in your approach. Life is unpredictable, and circumstances may change along the way. Be willing to adjust your goals as needed and embrace the journey of growth and knowledge that comes with pursuing them.

Chapter 5
Growth

Growth encompasses ongoing learning, personal development, and self-awareness. It acknowledges that education extends beyond formal schooling. Embracing a mindset of continuous growth and improvement, actively seeking out opportunities to expand your knowledge, skills, and perspectives throughout your lifetime. This could involve reading books, taking courses, attending workshops, seeking mentorship, or engaging in experiential learning.

It's crucial to adopt a mindset that welcomes growth, which means venturing outside your comfort zone and entertaining opportunities for growth and development. Growth involves taking risks, overcoming obstacles, and embracing the discomfort that comes with pushing yourself to new heights. By doing so, you open yourself up to new perspectives, fresh insights, and transformative experiences that have the potential to enrich both your personal and professional life.

As you develop and formulate new attitudes, you exude the need to cultivate a positive relationship with yourself. This includes practicing self-love, accepting yourself unconditionally, embracing your strengths and weaknesses, and treating yourself with kindness and compassion. Creating a routine for self-care practices and setting personal time aside for yourself helps you to relax and refocus. This will also help you to shift your vibration to a calm state where you can readily welcome your new reality. Self-care allows you to recognize your worth and value as a person. It reinforces you to be independent of external validation or achievements.

With this deeper understanding of self, you now establish the need to set and maintain healthy boundaries in your relationships and endeavors. You are able to identify your limits and recognize your triggers. Establishing these boundaries will empower you to prioritize your needs, values, and goals. By honoring them, you're agreeing to protect your well-being and autonomy, regardless of what your present looks like. Growth has no boundaries, so be patient with yourself as you adjust and transition to the new you.

Chapter 6
Relationships

Reformulating yourself invites you to cultivate and rebuild meaningful connections openly. Cultivating these relationships involves active listening, empathy, and mutual respect, as well as being present and supportive in times of need. A supportive network will provide you with a sense of belonging, allowing you to gain clarity on your purpose and vision. Surround yourself with people who uplift, inspire, and contribute to your overall well-being. It's important to foster relationships around trust, authenticity, and reciprocity where all involved feel valued and respected.

Remain knowing that while nurturing these newly formulated relationships is important, it's equally essential to maintain the boundaries you serve to protect your emotional, physical, and mental well-being, as well as to safeguard your values, priorities, and personal space. Set clear intentions and boldly communicate your needs and limits openly and assertively while also respecting the boundaries of others.

Though Rekindling relationships may not always be necessary or smooth, conflicts and differences are inevitable. You must develop an attitude toward listening to understand.

In any relationship, it calls for your time and effort to practice effective communication and your ability to navigate conflicts constructively. It may require you to have empathy and mutual respect, as well as be present and supportive in times of need.

Being present and supportive requires you to be open-minded with a wide range of possibilities and understanding. Though you may or may not agree with what the other party represents, they should feel comfortable voicing their opinion with you. You should be equally confident in commenting or not, depending on the situation. Each person has the right to their opinion, and points of view are generally up to one's knowledge and understanding.

Boundaries are the barriers in place to protect you from your insecurities. They are footprints and promises to yourself, voguing with confidence for change. It's common ground for both you and the other party to witness the changes and dedication you have toward becoming the better version of yourself. It takes willpower and growth to fully embrace, cultivate, activate, and maintain these boundaries. Over time, your muscles become stronger and your focus allows you to step into the beginning of your new reality.

Chapter 7

Health and Well-being

You must maintain and keep a healthy lifestyle. Engaging in physical activities not only strengthens muscles but also boosts mood and enhances overall well-being. Proper nutrition is important for optimal functioning and supporting energy levels. During transformation and beyond, you need to maintain a positive mindset. Your mental health serves as the foundation for processing shifts effectively, requiring you to remain firmly grounded and focused. Your mind is wired to protect you and keep you within the walls of your comfort. You must push past those barriers and recognize patterns you need to adjust or eliminate; your mind will try to block you from making these changes. If you're not focused on your ideals, you could be tricked into thinking you made progressions while simultaneously making excuses and justifications for not mindfully doing the work for transformation. Holding a clear vision for the future eliminates the fear factors and projections of others manipulating your energy. Set aside quiet time and get familiarized with your thoughts. Get to know yourself on a deeper level.

QUESTIONS...????

1. Whose voice are you hearing?
_____
_____

2. Are those thoughts mine?
_____
_____

3. Do the thoughts I'm having align with my future?
_____
_____

4. Why am I having these thoughts?
_____
_____
_____

5. What steps do I need to take to make the necessary changes?
_____
_____
_____

6. What routine do I need to eliminate or add?

_____

_____

_____

_____

_____

Having a clear mind before making any decisions is important. Practicing mindfulness and breath work aids in being present, enhancing your journey and continual progress. A less cluttered Mind allows you to make impactful decisions without the weight of future pressures or current burdens. This allows you to focus on daily problem-solving and reducing stress. Seeking professional guidance is recommended for a more effective individual structure.

Stress management is crucial for promoting your physical, mental health and spiritual life. Therefore, it is essential to develop healthy coping mechanisms to deal with stressors. You must acknowledge that the burdens are still there and that you need effective strategies to deal with them. Engaging in activities that promote relaxation and mindfulness, such as meditation, yoga, or spending time in nature, can help alleviate stress and improve mental resilience. By prioritizing self-care and implementing stress-reducing techniques, you can safeguard your mental health and enhance overall well-being.

Having an aware mind aids you in acknowledging and processing emotions healthily. You cultivate emotional intelligence that allows you to express your feelings openly, you release blame and give yourself compassion, and you nurture your relationships positively. Operating from an unconscious program, we tend to ignore the negative part of our emotions, which also hinders blockages for overcoming the darker aspect of self; you must fully embrace your reality and allow yourself to feel all emotions, implement the strategies you created to navigate those feelings and channel them to a more self-fulfilling outcome.

Mindfulness heightens your physical sensation. With a clearer understanding and connection to self, you're able to sense cues from the body and easily recognize discomforts. This could involve knowing when your body needs rest, nourishment, or relaxation. Listening to your body allows you to attune to signs of discomfort and imbalance with your energy. It draws attention to your level of comfort and discomfort in different atmospheres. Serving as a safeguard for your well-being. A full understanding of your body mechanism allows you an impactful transition with resilience and grace.

1. How do you handle stress?

_____
_____
_____
_____

2. What are your coping mechanisms?

_____
_____
_____
_____

3. What strategies or practices can help you navigate through tough times

_____
_____
_____
_____

(remember: being consistent with your practices will become natural over time)

Chapter 8

Resilience

Resilience is not about avoiding challenges but about building the inner strength and resourcefulness to thrive in the face of adversity. Resilience is a muscle you develop and strengthen over time. You cultivate mental and emotional fortitude to embrace Failures and challenges as opportunities for improvement and growth rather than seeing them as an obstacle. You face setbacks, failures and challenges with a positive mindset and determination to overcome them.

The stress-coping mechanism you have in place will assist you when navigating these waters. Understanding that your past is just as important as your future, you find value in identifying the lessons in your failures.

Ask yourself: Current reflections.

1. What can I learn from this experience?

_____
_____
_____
_____

2. How can I apply these lessons to future endeavors?

_____
_____
_____
_____

3. How will these lessons alter my thinking?

_____
_____
_____
_____

4. How can I protect myself if needed moving forward?

_____
_____
_____
_____

5. In what areas do I need to broaden my knowledge?

_____
_____
_____
_____

Failure is not a reflection of your worth; what matters is how you emerge and implement your knowledge after the lesson. It's an opportunity for growth and improvement.

Cultivate flexibility in your thinking and behavior to adapt to changing circumstances. When faced with unexpected challenges, be open to adjusting your approach and finding alternative solutions. Adaptability allows you to thrive in unpredictable situations. If you are stamping on new grounds, don't hesitate to lean on your support network.

Own your actions and decisions, whether they lead to success or failure. By taking responsibility for your choices, you empower yourself to make better decisions in the future and build trust and credibility with others. Treat yourself with the same empathy and understanding that you would offer to a friend facing similar challenges. Self-compassion fosters resilience by nurturing a positive self-image and inner strength.

Set realistic expectations as you reflect and be strategical with your coping mechanism to prevent feelings of exhaustion. Keep challenges in perspective by focusing on the bigger picture and reminding yourself of your values, strengths, and long-term goals. Maintaining a sense of perspective helps you navigate adversity resiliently and determined.

Cultivating these practices in your daily routine empowers you with the ability to bounce back stronger from adversity. The gift of present (presence) allows you the ability to tap into the past, review your encounters and make alignment and connections with the possible outcome for tomorrow (future). A setback could be merely an hour of correction as it could be years of repetition. Your empowerment comes in knowing, and the bounce back begins once you start adjusting. Time and patience are key.

Chapter 9
Living Authentically

Embrace who you truly are and align your actions, decisions, and relationships with your core values, beliefs, and principles. You have a clear understanding of self and what really matters to you. Your values serve as a compass, guiding your decisions and actions in alignment with your authentic self. Your understanding of living with purpose will guide you to participate in activities that matter to the heart.

Act with integrity by aligning your behavior with your values. Consistently living according to your principles builds trust and authenticity in your relationships and strengthens your sense of self-respect and confidence.

Embrace your uniqueness and dare to express yourself authentically, even if it means being vulnerable or facing criticism. Authenticity requires the willingness to show up as your genuine self, without pretense or masks, in both your personal and professional life.

Accept yourself fully, including your strengths, weaknesses, quirks, and imperfections. Embrace your humanity and recognize that no one is perfect. Self-acceptance frees you from the need for external validation and allows you to live with greater authenticity and inner peace.

Your boundaries allow you to protect your authenticity and well-being. Respecting your boundaries empowers you to honor your authenticity and maintain healthy connections with others. Surround yourself with people who accept and appreciate you for who you are. Cultivate relationships based on authenticity, mutual respect, and genuine connection. Authentic relationships provide a supportive environment for personal growth and self-expression.

Find creative outlets for self-expression that resonate with your authentic voice. Whether it's through art, writing, music, or other forms of creativity, expressing yourself authentically fosters a deeper connection with your inner truth. It allows you to share your unique perspective with the world.

Practicing mindfulness allows you to create thoughts, emotions, and actions in the present moment. Being mindful enables you to make conscious choices aligned with your authentic self rather than reacting impulsively or conforming to external expectations.

Horn in on your growth evolution, and allow yourself the flexibility to evolve, adapt, and refine your beliefs and values when needed as you gain new insights and experiences. Living authentically is not about rigidly adhering to a fixed identity but about embracing the process of self-discovery and growth as your knowledge increases.

Living authentically is a journey of self-discovery, self-expression, and self-empowerment. By honoring your values, embracing your uniqueness, and expressing yourself authentically, you can live a life that is true to who you are at the core.

Chapter 10
Making a Positive Impact

Recognizing your capability to contribute to the well-being of others and the world around you. Living with purpose, empathy, and a commitment to making a difference, even in the face of challenges. Adopt a service-oriented mindset, focus on change and uplifting others. Seek ways to use your time, talents, and resources to support those in need, whether it's through volunteering, mentoring, or acts of kindness in your daily life.

Stand up for causes you believe in and advocate for justice when necessary. By engaging within your community, you can collaborate with like-minded individuals and organizations to create positive change at the local level.

Coming in with others helps you deepen your empathy and compassion. You seek to understand their experiences, perspectives, and needs. Empathy allows you to connect with people on a deeper level, recognize their humanity, and respond with kindness and support.

Stay resilient and persevere in your efforts, maintaining a steadfast commitment to your values and goals. Be a role model for others by embodying the values and principles you wish to see in the world. Being open and vulnerable allows others to see that the aim is not perfection; it's radically deciding for change and actively working and making visible progress.

Acknowledge and celebrate the progress you make and the impact you create, no matter how small. Recognize that positive change takes time and effort, and every act of kindness and compassion contributes to a brighter, more compassionate world. Stay curious and open-minded, staying informed about emerging issues and opportunities for positive change.

About the Author

Moya Martin, affectionately known as Moya, was born and raised on the picturesque island of Jamaica. Growing up in such a vibrant and culturally rich environment, she developed a unique blend of charm, creativity, and business acumen—qualities that have fueled her impressive success.

With over a decade of experience in the real estate industry, Moya has been deeply committed to growth and redevelopment, consistently pushing the boundaries of excellence. Her passion for innovation and dedication to her craft have established her as a respected leader in the field. Now, Moya is excited to share her wealth of knowledge and insights through illustration and book publishing, with the goal of inspiring, educating, and empowering others.

Outside of her professional pursuits, Moya enjoys producing music, exploring new destinations with her family, and creating delicious meals in the kitchen. Her diverse interests and talents reflect her dynamic personality and her zest for life.

Stay tuned for Moya's upcoming publications, where her expertise and creativity come together to inspire readers around the world.

www.ingramcontent.com/pod-product-compliance
Lightning Source LLC
LaVergne TN
LVHW051040070526
838201LV00066B/4873